When Your Pet Dies:
Helping Yourself with Grief

When Your Pet Dies:
Helping Yourself with Grief

David R. Tullock

Parson's Porch Books
121 Holly Trail, NW
Cleveland, TN 37311

Copyright (C) 2011 by David Russell Tullock

ISBN: Softcover 978-1-936912-02-5

All rights reserved. No part of this book may be reproduced or transmitted in any form or by any means, electronic or mechanical, including photocopying, recording, or by any information storage and retrieval system, without permission in writing from the publisher.

This book was printed in the United States of America.

To order additional copies of this book, contact:
Parson's Porch Books
1-423-475-7308
www.parsonsporch.com

Table of Contents

An Old Friend..................................7

A Broader Framework of Loss....................10

Myths About Grief......................14

Other Pet Loss Myths............................... 23

My Grief is Unique..................... 31

The Grief Journey........................46

Other Things to Expect. 51

Helping with Pet Loss................................58

How Am I Doing?........................60

Other Places to Find Support......................65

Helping a Friend .... .67

Children and Pet Loss.................................71

A Pet's Prayer...............................74

An Old Friend

The old dog lay quietly on the soft, white blanket looking up with trusting eyes at his master of thirteen years. The once proud and strong Dalmatian was now feeble and mostly deaf. The limbs that once trotted powerfully up the driveway to guide arriving cars to the house, now shook uncontrollably. The intelligent and gentle eyes that looked out from the sleek head were now mostly filled with confusion and great pain.

The old dog's master and friend held up the syringe filled with the clear, pink solution and looked at his long-time companion. "I'm going to miss you old friend," he whispered. He placed a hand on top of the broad soft head and gently stroked the great dog's velvet ears. The tail thumped weakly in response. Then with a precision that comes with long years of experience, he inserted the needle expertly into the old dog's vein and slowly depressed the plunger. A sob caught in his throat as he watched his friend crumple into the folds of the blanket. He sat and watched the chest rise and fall as he murmured gently to the dying dog. As his old protector and companion took his last breath, he placed his stethoscope to the now silent chest and listened for a moment. Then he folded a portion of the blanket over the lifeless body.

He let the other dogs in so that they might understand the new status of the household. No one knows what a dog really thinks and feels, but he felt that doing this was important. Two of the dogs ran around as if nothing new had transpired. But the smallest of them all, the one that had grown up with the old Dalmatian, lay down quietly next to the inert body and rested his tiny muzzle on the great dog's paw.

Silently he dug a grave in the wet ground, his tears mingling freely with the rain. He had picked this final resting spot carefully, placing it between two other old friends, a beloved dog and cat that the old Dalmatian had spent many happy years with.

It had not been an easy decision. He had counseled and empathized with many of his clients who had wrestled with the same choice. He himself had agonized over it for a long time. But he finally knew that he needed to help his friend escape the constant pain that all of his veterinary training and years of experience could not erase.

As the last shovelful of dirt was placed over the grave, he felt deeply saddened that he'd never again gaze upon the soft, wise eyes, but knew in his heart that his old friend was finally at peace.

The act of grieving is often complicated by feelings that perhaps we should not be "over-reacting" to the death of "just" a pet. Many friends and family members don't understand what the pet has meant to us in life and don't empathize with these very real and deep feelings. If you are having trouble coping, would like more information about the grief process, or are considering euthanasia, please call. We're here to help you.

A Broader Framework of Loss

The experience of mourning losses in our lives is much more common than we often stop to realize. When we hear the word grief we normally associate it with death. We should note, however, that there are a variety of losses that are a basic part of living. How we deal with other losses in our life influences how we experience the death of our pets. There are basically four areas of loss.

The Loss of a Person

The death of someone you love is often the most intense form of relationship loss. However, there are a variety of relationship losses. Separation, divorce, and relocation are but a few examples of relationship losses. In addition, aging and illness may result in the loss of a relationship with a person in the form we once knew it.

Mitchell and Anderson, in their book, *All Our Losses, All Our Griefs*, described the loss of relationship when they wrote the following:

> Relationship loss is the ending of opportunities to relate oneself to, talk with, share experiences with, make love to, touch, settle issues with, fight with, and otherwise be in the emotional and physical presence of a particular human being.

The Loss of Some Aspect of Self

This area of loss exists within one's self. Many external losses that occur, like death, are accompanied by a "loss of self." The natural tendency is to define oneself by the relationships, roles, and ideas to which one is attached. Examples of loss of some aspect of self are loss of:

* ideas, hopes and dreams
* health and/or body function
* self-esteem and positive self-attitude
* belief system or faith
* role, such as spouse, parent or friend

The reality that much overlapping and compounding of losses are easy to observe as we consider these losses related to self. The death of a loved one may result in a loss of some aspect of self.

The Loss of External Objects

People naturally have meaningful attachments to some external objects such as their home, land, or special possessions. While we often replace material possessions, that fact alone does not negate the experience with loss and grief. The replacement is never quite the same as the original. Anyone who has experienced the loss of valued objects to fire, flood, or theft can certainly attest to the significance of this type of loss.

Developmental Losses

Loss is present from the moment of birth until the moment of death. In a real sense, life is a series of losses. Examples of these kind of losses are:

* Growing from childhood into adolescence
* A child moving away to college or getting married
* Retirement
* Moving into a nursing home

Though expected, these developmental losses are often traumatic for people. We would never want to assume that just because a loss is expected that it is easy to deal with.

What other losses in your life have occurred because of your pet's death?

Myths About Grief

What a wonderful responsibility we take on when we bring a pet into our lives. With the help and guidance from veterinarians, we provide a loving, safe and healthy environment for our pets who share everything with us. Pets see us through marriages, divorces, and the birth of children. Pets endure separation and welcome us back as if we'd been away forever. They are the best pals we have for accepting us as we are.

But one day, that constant will become one of our losses. And when the kind face and acceptance we used to turn to is gone, where do we go for comfort?

One of the most difficult and important parts of grief and loss is seeking to understand what has happened and that what you are feeling is all right. Your sense of loss may encompass your life and that is all right. You have that right to grieve and you can take as much time as you need. In a busy and demanding world, the trick is to take the time.

The sense of loss is overwhelming. You are grieving. Your need to mourn is both difficult and necessary.

You have begun a journey that is often frightening, painful, and sometimes lonely. No words, written or spoken, can take away the pain you feel now.

It is important that you become an active participant in your healing. Perhaps people have treated you like a patient. By definition, the word "patient" implies that you are a person who has a malady that someone else will heal. To rediscover continued meaning in life after the loss, avoid thinking of yourself as a "passive patient" being treated for your pain. Rather, see yourself as an "active participant" in your grief journey. Embrace your pain and learn from your experience.

One thing to understand at the outset of your journey is: you cannot heal without mourning or expressing your grief outwardly. Denying your grief, running from it, or minimizing it only seems to make it more confusing and overwhelming. To lessen your hurt, you must embrace it.

In his book, *A Grief Observed*, C.S. Lewis wrote about his experience after the death of his wife. He stated:

An odd by-product of my loss is that I'm aware of being an embarrassment to everyone I meet... Perhaps the bereaved ought to be isolated in special settlements like lepers."

As he teaches us from his experience, Lewis describes how society often tends to make the bereaved feel intense shame and embarrassment about the feeling of grief. "Safe harbors" are sometimes difficult to find for ones who are grieving. The support group of which you now are a member will provide you a safe place to mourn.

Simon Stephens suggests that grief only becomes a tolerable and creative experience when love enables it to be shared with someone who really understands.

To heal sometimes requires clarifying some misunderstandings about grief. As you read some of the common myths about mourning and grieving you may discover some of them which you, or others who give you support, have embraced. The questions which follow the description of each myth will help you explore how these misconceptions may be influencing your grief. Answer each question candidly and use the response as a tool to understand your personal grief journey.

Myth #1: Grief and mourning are the same experience.

The majority of people tend to use the words "grieving" and "mourning" synonymously. An important distinction exists between them. Grief is the set of thoughts and emotions one feels when one experiences a loss. Grief is the internal meaning given to the experience of bereavement.

In contrast, mourning is when you take the grief on the inside and express it outside yourself. Another way of defining mourning is "sharing your grief outside of yourself." In other words, when you cry, talk about the person who has died, or celebrate the anniversary date of the person you loved, you are mourning.

After your pet dies, friends may encourage you to "keep your grief to yourself." Healing will only come when these bottled up feelings are expressed publicly in the presence of understanding, caring persons who will not judge you. At times, of course, you will grieve alone, but expressing your grief outside yourself is necessary if you are to move forward in your grief journey.

Have you been the victim of Myth #1: Grief and

mourning are the same experiences? Yes ____ No ____ If so, how will your new awareness influence you in your grief journey?

Myth #2: The experience of grief and mourning progress in predictable and orderly stages.

Probably you have already heard about the "stages of grief." This approach to dealing with dying, grief, and mourning is appealing but inaccurate. The experience of grief is not orderly and predictable. Attempts have been made to replace fear and lack of understanding with the security that everyone grieves by going through the same stages. If only it were true.

Although the experience of grief is universal - everyone grieves after a loss, grief is also individualistic - each ones personality plays a key role in how one expresses ones grief. As a part of your healing process, the thoughts and feelings you will experience will be totally unique to you.

Have you been the victim of Myth # 2: The experience of grief and mourning progress in predictable and orderly stages? Yes____ No____ If so, how will your new awareness influence your grief journey?

Myth #3: Move away from grief, not toward it.

Our society often encourages people to move away from grief instead of toward it. The result is that too many bereaved people either grieve in isolation or attempt to run away from their grief through various means.

Bereaved persons who continue to express grief outwardly are often viewed as "weak," "crazy," or "self-pitying." The subtle message is "shape up and get on with life." The reality is disturbing: far too many people view grief as something to be overcome rather than experience.

Remember, society will often encourage you to prematurely move away from your grief. You must continually remind yourself that leaning toward the pain will facilitate the eventual healing.

Have you been a victim of Myth #3: Move away from grief, not toward it? Yes____ No____ If so, how will your new awareness influence your grief journey?

Myth #4: Following the death of someone loved, the goal should be to "get over" your grief as soon as possible.

You may have already been asked, "Are you over it yet?" Or even worse, "Well, you should be over it by now." For someone to think that you can "get over" your grief is ludicrous!

I prefer to use the term reconciliation. Reconciliation does not mean that you will get over your grief. It means growing through it.

You do not "get over " your grief. As you become willing to embrace the work of your mourning, however, you can and will become reconciled to it. Unfortunately, when the people around you think you have to "resolve" your grief, they set you up to fail.

Have you been a victim of Myth #4: Following the death of someone you loved, the goal should be to "get over" your grief as soon as possible? Yes____ No____ If so, how will your new awareness influence your grief journey?

Myth #5: Tears expressing grief are only a sign of weakness.

Tears of grief are often associated with personal inadequacy and weakness. The worst thing you can do, however, is to allow judgment to prevent yourself from crying. While your tears may result in a feeling of helplessness for friends, family, and caregivers, you must not let others stifle your need to mourn openly.

People may directly or indirectly try to prevent your tears out of a desire to protect you and themselves from pain. You may have heard comments like "Tears won't bring him back." or "He wouldn't want you to cry." Yet crying is nature's way of releasing internal tension in your body, and it allows you to communicate a need to be comforted.

Be constantly aware that the expression of tears is not a sign of weakness. Your capacity to share tears is an indication of your willingness to do the work of mourning.

Have you been the victim of Myth # 5: Tears expressing grief are only a sign of weakness? Yes____ No____ If so, how will your new awareness influence you grief journey?

Please remember that the list of myths about grief and mourning is not exclusive. List below any other "grief myth" you have encountered since the death of someone loved. How do these myths influence your grief journey?

Other Pet Loss Myths

"I didn't know anyone else felt as deeply as I do towards animals" a number of people have confided in me. When it comes to your love of animals, you may not be as alone as you think! Some pet owners are extraordinarily attached and dedicated to their animal companions. So when their good (or best) friends die - or otherwise leave their lives - they are heartbroken and sometimes devastated.

Since more and more animal lovers are "coming out of the closet," fewer animal lovers are feeling as alone with their intense pet-related grief. More and more animal lovers are openly talking about their deep bonds with their furred, feathered, finned, and scaled friends. Peoples' attitudes towards pet loss have really changed in the last 40 years - especially in the last decade. Despite growing enlightenment, misperceptions about pet loss still persist. These myths hinder healthy mourning. Here are some of the myths followed by the realities.

Myth: People who experience intense grief over the

loss or anticipated loss of a pet are crazy, weird, or strange.

Reality: Individuals who say this, or believe this, are judgmental. Experiencing powerful feelings of distress over the loss of a loved animal companion is, usually, normal and healthy. People who have strong feelings about the loss of a pet have them because they are capable of intimate attachments and deep emotional bonding. This is something to be proud of, not something to put down.

Myth: Pet loss is insignificant when compared to the loss of human life. To mourn the loss of a pet devalues the importance of human relationships.

Reality: The loss of a beloved animal companion can be as emotionally significant, even more significant, than the loss of a human friend or relative. People are capable of simultaneously loving and caring about both animals and humans. One doesn't have to detract from the other.

Myth: It is best to replace the lost pet as quickly as possible. This will ease the pain of loss.

Reality: Animal companions cannot be "replaced." They are not interchangeable. They are all separate, different individuals with unique personalities. People need to feel emotionally ready to get another pet before they can successfully adopt a new animal into their hearts and family. Some people attempt to avoid the mourning process by rushing out to get a "replacement" pet. This isn't good for people or for the pets.

Myth: It is best to mourn alone. This is a way to be strong and independent, and not burden others with your problems. Besides, you need to protect yourself from being ridiculed for loving and missing your special animal friend.

Reality: It takes courage to reach out to others. Mourners can greatly benefit by the empathy, caring, and understanding of supportive others. But be selective about where you turn to for help since some people do not take pet loss seriously.

Myth: Resolution and closure (a bringing to an end; conclusion) to mourning occurs when you have succeeded in having only pleasant memories of your pet.

Reality: It is rare that anyone ever achieves complete resolution or closure to a profound loss. One is left with psychological scars, if not with incompletely healed wounds. It is unrealistic to expect that you will one day be left with only pleasant memories. Besides, being left with only pleasant memories is one-sided and doesn't present a balanced view of reality - not a goal that would be healthy or valuable to pursue. One cannot fully appreciate pleasant memories unless one has unpleasant memories to contrast them with.

Myth: It is selfish to euthanize your pet.

Reality: Euthanasia is a compassionate and humane way to end the intense suffering or declining quality of life of a companion animal. Viewed in this context, it would be selfish to unnecessarily prolong the suffering of a seriously ill or injured animal. Ask yourself this: Whose needs and best interests are being served - those of the owner or animal companion?

Myth: The best way to cope with unpleasant loss related feelings and thoughts is to suppress and bury them. Keep busy so as to not dwell on your troubles.

Reality: Upsetting feelings and thoughts will not just go away. They will, instead, go underground (become unconscious) and later return - causing you problems. Achieve a balance by thinking and talking about what is upsetting you when you are able, but avoid overdoing it. Know your limits.

Myth: When a person starts talking with sadness about missing his/her pet it is best to redirect their attention to pleasant memories they have about the pet.

Reality: This may be an example where the listener has good intentions but will produce bad effects by his/her response. People who talk about their unpleasant feelings are looking for a receptive ear. Redirecting the conversation or changing the subject reflects the discomfort of the listener rather than the needs of the mourner.

Myth: Time heals all wounds. Just give it enough time and you will no longer feel so bad.

Reality: Time by itself does not heal the pain of grief related loss. It's what you do with your time that matters. Some people suffer the harsh or even traumatic effects of pet loss for years, or even a lifetime. A successful course of mourning requires intentional hard work.

Myth: The best way to protect yourself from the pain of pet loss is to not get another pet.

Reality: Depriving yourself of an animal companion is a very high price to pay to help insure yourself against experiencing another painful loss. Instead, you may wish to summon up the courage to put in the effort necessary to work through your mourning related psychological issues. Despite your pains of loss you can still look forward to one day sharing happiness, pleasure, and joy, with a new and unique animal companion. It is an unfortunate fact that one of the prices we pay for loving so deeply is to suffer deeply when the bonds with our cherished animal friends are broken.

Myth: Children handle pet loss rather easily. That which occurs in childhood has little carryover into adult life.

Reality: Just because children do not react as overtly as adults, or communicate directly with words, does not mean they aren't experiencing strong reactions inside. Not infrequently, the loss of a pet (whether by death or another cause) is the first significant loss the child will have experienced. The profound effects of this loss, and how parents or other caregivers handle it, might reverberate in the child for many years to come.

Myth: It is best to protect children from the upsetting truth of what has happened to their pet.

Reality: Some parents/caregivers think they are helping their child - sparing them pain - when they do not tell him or her that their pet has died. They sometimes make up a story that they gave the pet away or that the pet ran away. What the parents don't realize in doing this is that through their well intentioned lies and deceits they are undermining the trust their child has in them, and paradoxically, causing the child much more pain in the long run. Some children, for example, will unfairly blame themselves for their pet "running away."

Myth: Pets don't mourn for other pets.

Reality: Some companion animals develop strong bonds with other pets in the household and they will show some of the same kinds of symptoms of mourning as people do - such as loss of appetite, "searching" for the missed loved one, and acting depressed.

Myth: Pet loss is something you should be able to "get over" on your own. There is no need for someone to see a professional pet loss counselor in order to deal with this.

Reality: Some people have a self-interested need for you to "get over" your pet related mourning as soon as possible, before you are ready to do so. They feel uncomfortable with your distress. If, for example, you broke an arm you would go to a physician to get help. So why wouldn't you see a human-animal bond specialist to get help for a broken heart? This can be seen as an investment in your mental health and peace of mind.

Overcoming these myths can be difficult - for maintaining these beliefs does have some advantages. But those who don't work through their feelings and reactions about mourning are likely to experience a variety of physical, intellectual, emotional, interpersonal, and spiritual symptoms later. It's very hard to learn new and healthier ways of feeling, thinking, and behaving, but the many benefits are worth the effort.

My Grief is Unique

Perhaps the nicest thing about being human is that we are all different. No two people are exactly alike. As a result, your grief journey will not be the same as someone else. Your grief is unique.

Despite what you may hear, you will do the "work of mourning" in your own special way. Be careful not to compare your experience with that of other people. Just accept a "one-day-at-a-time" approach. Doing so allows you to mourn at your own pace.

What factors influence your personal grief? Let's explore them!

Factor #1: The Nature of the Relationship with the Pet Which Died.

Your relationship with the pet which died is different than that pet's relationship with anyone else. For example, you may have been extremely close. Perhaps you loved the pet who died but it seemed that you always had disagreements and

When Your Pet Dies

conflict in your relationship. Or, perhaps you were completely miserable in the relationship. Whatever the circumstances, you are the best person to describe and work toward understanding your relationship with your pet.

Think about your relationship with you pet who died and then respond candidly to the following questions:

1. How attached were you to this pet? Describe how this attachment was reflected in your behaviors toward each other.

2. Were there times you had conflicts with this pet? Yes____ No____ If so, describe the nature of those conflicts.

3. Do you feel that you have any "unfinished business" in your relationship with this pet? Yes____ No____ If so, describe the nature of the "unfinished business."

4. Can you recall one of the times you felt very close to this pet? Yes____ No____ Please describe.

5. What special memories will you always have about this pet?

Factor #2: Circumstances Surrounding the Death.

The unique circumstances surrounding the death of your pet can have an impact on your journey into grief. For example, was the death anticipated or sudden and unexpected? How old was the pet who died? Do you feel you might have been able to prevent the death.

Write your responses to the following questions to help you better understand the unique circumstances surrounding the nature of the death.

1. How did your pet die?

2. How old was the pet who died? How does the age of the pet affect your grief?

3. Was the death anticipated, or was it sudden and unexpected? What influence does this fact have on your grief?

4. Do you have any sense that you should have been able to prevent the death? Yes____ No____ If so, write out your thoughts and feelings about this.

Factor #3: Circumstances Surrounding your Support System.

Mourning requires the outside support of other human beings in order for you to heal. Without a stabilizing support system of at least one other person, the odds are you will have difficulty in doing the work of mourning. To heal requires an environment of empathy, caring, and gentle encouragement.

Sometimes other people may have a support system when, in fact, you do not. For example, you may have family members or friends who live near you, but you discover that they have little compassion for, or lack patience with you and your grief. If so, a vital ingredient to your healing is missing.

You may have friends and family who have some friends or relatives who are supportive for a relatively short period of time after the death. In the weeks that follow the death, however, this support drops off quickly.

Even when you have a viable support system in place, are you able to accept the support that is available to you? If you are ashamed about you need to mourn, you may end up isolating yourself from the very people who would most like to walk with you in your time of grief.

Write your responses to the following questions so you will better understand the unique nature of your support system.

1. Do you have a stabilizing support system available? Yes____ No____ If so, who makes up your support system for understanding your need to mourn?

2. Are there some people in your life whom you wish were more supportive, but who are not? Yes____ No____ If so, who are these people?

3. Why is it difficult for them to "be with you" in your grief?

4. Does physical distance from people influence your

support system? Yes____ No____ Explain.
5. Are you able to accept support from the people who want to be helpful? Yes____ No____ If not, why are you unable to accept support?

Factor #4: Your Unique Personality.

Your unique personality will be reflected in your grief. For example, if you are quiet by nature, you may express your grief quietly. If you are outgoing, you may be more expressive with your grief.

Your responses to other losses or crises in your life will also probably be consistent with how you respond to the death of someone loved. If you like to remain distant or run away from crises, you may do the same thing now. If you, however, have always confronted crises head-on and openly expressed your thoughts and feelings, you may now follow that pattern of behavior.

Other personality influences, such as your self-esteem, values, and beliefs, also impact your response to the death. In addition, any long-term problems with depression or anxiety may influence your response at this time.

Write your responses to the following questions so you will better understand how unique factors in your personality influence your grief journey.

1. What are some adjectives you would use to describe yourself?

2. How is your unique personality influencing your journey into grief?

3. How have you responded to previous losses or crises in your life?

4. Are you responding in a similar way now, or does it seem different than in the past? Explain.

5. What has your self-esteem been like over the years?

6. How is your self-esteem right now?

7. Have you had previous problems with long-term depression or anxiety in your life Yes____ No____
If so, how might yo influence your response to this death?

Factor #5: The Unique Personality of the Pet which Died.

Just as your unique personality is reflected in your grief journey, so, too, is the personality of the pet who died. For example, if that pet was always a soothing, stabilizing influence within the family, your family may not be as close as prior to the death. In contrast, if the pet was never easy to be around, you may find yourself experiencing ambivalent feelings about the loss. Whatever your feeling are, talk about them openly. The key is finding someone you can trust who will not judge your feelings.

Respond to the following questions so you can better understand how the unique personality of the person who died influences your grief journey.

1. What was the personality like of the pet who died?

2. What are some adjectives you would use to describe this pet?

3. What roles did the pet play in your life (for example, best friend, competitor, stabilizer, disrupter, lover) and how was this role influenced by his or her personality?

4. What personality traits did this pet have that you enjoyed the most in your relationship? What times can you recall when these traits were expressed by your pet?

5. What personality traits did this pet have that you did not always care for in your relationship? Do you remember a specific time when these negative traits were expressed by this pet? Yes____ No____ If so, please describe below.

Factor #6: Your Own Cultural Background.

Cultural influences can be an important influence on how you express your grief. Your family probably had cultural traditions that were passed down through the generations. For example, families with German heritage sometimes demonstrate a more stoic, stiff upper lip approach to loss. An Italian family might be more expressive with feelings.

While you may not be consciously aware of these cultural influences, taking time to explore these questions might create some new awareness for you.

1. What is your cultural background?

2. Does this background influence your mourning? Yes____ No____ If so, how?

3. Does this cultural background help or hinder you in your work of mourning? Yes____ No____ Please explain.

Factor #7: Your Religious or Spiritual Background.

Your personal belief system can have a tremendous impact on your journey into grief. You may discover that your religious or spiritual is deepened, renewed, or changed as a result of your loss. Or you may find yourself questioning your previously held belief system as part of you work of mourning.

Mistakenly, people may think that with faith, there is no need to mourn. If you support this premise, you will set yourself up to grieve internally, but not mourn externally. Having faith does not mean you do not need to mourn. It does mean having the courage to allow yourself to mourn.

With the death of your pet comes a search for meaning. you will find yourself re-evaluating your life based on this loss. You will need to find someone who is willing to listen to you as you explore your religious or spiritual values, question your attitude toward life, and renew your resources for living.

1. What are the religious or spiritual teachings with which you grew up?

2. What is your current religious, spiritual or philosophical belief system as it relates to life and death?

3. How has this death impacted your belief system?

4. Do you have any "Why?" questions right now? Yes____ No____ If so, what are they?

5. Do you have a support system of people around you to validate your belief system? Yes____ No____ If so, identify this support system and explore what this means to you right now?

6. How do you see your religious or spiritual belief system playing a part in your healing process? Yes____ No____ Please explain.

Factor #8: Other Crises or Stresses in Your Life.

The death of your pet can often bring to the surface what are formally called "secondary losses." An individual loss seldom occurs in isolation. You may experience the loss of financial security, the loss of a sense of future, the loss of some long-time friends who abandon you in your grief, the loss of your home or perhaps the loss of your community. You also may be unemployed or experiencing strained family relationships. Take note that staying aware of how these other losses can and will influence your grief is very important.

Respond to the following questions to better understand how the other crises or stresses in your life influence your grief journey.

1. What other losses have come about in your life as

a result of this death?

2. How do you see these additional losses influencing your grief?

3. What other stresses or crises are a part of your life right now?

4. How do you see these additional stresses or crises influencing your grief?

5. What can you do right now to help yourself cope with these losses and stresses?

Factor #9: Your Gender.

Being a male or female can have an influence not only on your grief, but also on how people relate to you at this time. While being careful not to generalize, men are often encouraged and expected to "be strong" and restrained. Typically, men have more difficulty in allowing themselves to move toward painful feelings than women do.

Women sometimes experience difficulties in expressing feelings of anger. In contrast, men tend to be more quick to respond with explosive emotions. Because men are conditioned to be totally self-sufficient, they often have difficulty accepting outside support.

1. How does your gender influence the expression of your own grief?

2. Has your gender influenced how people support you in your grief? Yes____ No____ If so, how?

3. Do you see any advantage or disadvantage to being the gender that you are in experiencing your grief? Yes____ No____ If so, what are these advantages and disadvantages?

Factor #10: The Funeral Experience.

Decisions you make relating to the funeral can either help or hinder your personal grief experience. A funeral helps provide an appropriate setting that permits and encourages you to express your feelings. In other words, the funeral legitimizes the feelings related to the loss. The funeral also serves as a time to honor the pet who has died, bring you closer to others who can give you needed support, affirm that life goes on even in the face of death, and gives you a context of meaning related to your own religious background.

If you were unable to attend the funeral of the pet who died, or if the funeral was somehow minimized or distorted, you may find that this complicates your healing process. Be assured, however, that some things can still be done by you to help yourself heal.

Respond to the following questions:

1. Did you participate in a funeral for the pet who died? Yes____ No____ If so, did this help meet your needs?

2. Were you unable to participate in some kind of funeral for the pet who died? Yes____ No____ If not, how did you feel about that?

3. Do you feel a need to create any additional ritual that would help you with your grief? Yes____ No____ If so, what could you do to make this happen?

4. In what ways can you continue to ritualize the death of this pet?

The Grief Journey

Your pet has died. You are beginning a journey that is often frightening, painful and sometimes lonely. No word, written or spoken, can take away the pain you now feel. I hope, however, that these words will bring you some comfort and encouragement as you make a commitment to help yourself heal.

Perhaps someone has already said to you, "In time, you'll feel better." Actually, time alone has nothing to do with healing. To heal, you must be willing to learn about and understand the grief process and how it will affect you today, tomorrow and forever.

As scary as this may sound, you will never "get over" your grief. Instead, you will learn to live with it. This does not mean that you will never be happy again. On the contrary, many bereaved people who have moved toward healing find their lives even fuller and more meaningful than they were before the death of someone loved. If you allow yourself the time and compassion to mourn, if you truly work through your grief, you, too, will heal. You too will go on to find continued meaning in living and loving.

So, what can you expect in the weeks and months ahead? It depends. You see, grief is different for every person. It may also feel different for you now than it did if someone close to you died in years past. Grief is never the same twice.

While your grief is unique, it might help you to understand some of the most common emotions associated with grief:

Shock. You may feel dazed and stunned, especially during the time immediately following the death. This feeling is nature's way of protecting you from the overwhelming reality. You may experience heart palpitations, queasiness, stomach pains or dizziness. You may also find yourself crying hysterically, screaming angrily or even laughing. These behaviors help you survive during this extraordinary difficult time.

Confusion. After the death of your pet loved, you may feel a sense of ongoing confusion. It's like being in the midst of a wild, rushing river where you can't get hold of anything. Disconnected thoughts race through your mind and you may be unable to complete any tasks. As part of your confusion, you might also experience a sense of the dead person's presence or even have fleeting glimpses of the person across the room. I call this latter experience, which is very common and very normal, a "memory picture."

Anxiety. As your head and heart begin to miss the pet who died, you may naturally feel anxious. You may fear that you or others you love will die, too. You may doubt your ability to survive without the pet who died. You may feel anxious about everyday realities, such as work or finances. You may even panic as you think through the repercussions of this death.

Anger. Anger and its cousins hate, blame, terror, resentment, rage and jealousy are normal responses to the death of someone loved. With loss comes the desire to protest. Explosive emotions such as these provide the vehicle to do so. If feelings like these are part of your journey, be aware that you have two avenues for expressing them: outward or inward. The outward avenue leads to healing. The inward avenue does not. Critical to your healing is finding someone who doesn't judge you but allows you to feel whatever you feel.

Guilt. When your pet dies, it's natural to consider the "if-only's". If only I had died myself. If only I had told her to buckle her seatbelt. In only... The list goes on. You may feel guilty if you feel a sense of relief. This feeling is especially true if the death was after an extended illness or if there was some ambivalence in the relationship. While these feelings of guilt and regret are natural, they are sometimes not logical to those around you. But remember - thinking is logical. Feeling is not.

Sadness. Your pet has died and you hurt. Your full sense of loss will never occur all at once. Weeks or often months will pass before you are fully confronted with the depths of your sadness. This slow progression is good. You could not or should not tolerate all of your sadness at once. Your body, mind and spirit need time working together to allow you to embrace the depth of your loss. Be patient with yourself.

You may also experience physiological changes as part of your grief. Actually, one literal definition of the word "grievous" is causing physical suffering. You may also be shocked by how much your body responds to the impact of your loss. Among the most common physical responses to loss are trouble with sleeping and low energy. You may have trouble getting to sleep or you may wake up early in the morning and have trouble getting back to sleep. You may find yourself feeling tired more than usual.

Muscle aches and pains, shortness of breath, feelings of emptiness in your stomach, tightness in your throat or chest, digestive problems, sensitivity to noise, heart palpitations, queasiness, nausea, headaches, increased allergic reactions, changes in appetite, weight loss or gain, agitation and generalized tension - all are ways your body may react to the loss of someone loved.

Good self-care is important at this time. The stress of grief can suppress your immune system and make you more likely to experience physical problems. See a physician for specific physical symptoms that concern you.

Which of the above characteristics of grief has been most prevalent in your experience?

Other Things to Expect

There are some other things that some people have experienced in their grief journey. These things may or may not be a part of your grief experience. Let's explore some of them.

Time Distortion. "I don't know what day it is or what time it is." This kind of statement is not unusual when you are mourning. Sometimes, time moves quickly. At other times, time merely crawls. Your sense of the past and future also may seem to be frozen in place. You may lose track of what day or what month it is.

My experience with time distortion has been....

Obsessive Review. You may be aware that you are telling your story over and over again. In your grief journey, you may often review the events surrounding the death of your pet. You may sit for hours just thinking about days gone by. This normal process helps bring your head and heart together! Allow yourself time to do this. Blocking it out will not help you heal. Don't be angry with yourself

when you find yourself wanting to re-tell your story. Review is a powerful and necessary part of the hard work of mourning. Be compassionate with yourself.
Surround yourself with people who allow you to repeat whatever you need to tell again.

My experience with telling my experience over and over again is or has been...

Search for Meaning. Naturally, you try to make sense of why your pet died. You may find yourself asking questions like "Why him or her?" "Why this way?" "Why now?" Yes, it is O.K. to have questions. You are human and you are simply trying to understand your experience. You may or may not receive specific answers to your questions. Yet, you still need to give yourself permission to ask them.

Be aware that people may try to tell you not to ask questions about your personal search for meaning in your grief journey. Or worse yet, watch out for people who always try to have easy answers to your difficult questions. Most bereaved people do not find comfort in pat responses, neither will you. The healing comes in posing the questions in the first place, not just in finding answers.

What questions have you had concerning the death of your pet?

Transitional Objects. Transitional objects are belongings of your pet who died. They often can give you comfort. Objects such as clothing, books, or prized possessions can help you feel close to someone you miss so much. Some people try to distance themselves from these objects. This behavior fits with the tendency of our culture to move away from grief instead of toward it.

Remember - embrace the comfort provided by familiar objects. To do away with them too soon takes away a sense of security these belongings provide. Once you move toward reconciliation, you will probably be better able to decide what to do with them. Some things, however, you may want to keep forever.

What are your favorite objects of the pet who died and how have they helped comfort you?

Suicidal Thoughts. Thoughts that come and go about questioning if you want to go on living can be a normal part of your grief and mourning. You might say or think, "I'm not sure I'd mind if I didn't wake up in the morning." Often this thought is not so much an active wish to kill yourself as it is a wish to ease your pain.

To have these thoughts is normal. However, to make plans and take action to end your life is abnormal. Sometimes your body, mind, and spirit can hurt so much you wonder if you will ever feel alive again. If your thoughts of suicide take on planning and structure, make certain that you can get help immediately. Sometimes tunnel vision can prevent you from seeing choices. Please choose to go on living as you honor the memory of the person in your life who has died.

My experience with suicidal thoughts or the desire not to go on living is ...

Grief Attacks. "I was just sailing along pretty well, when out of nowhere came this overwhelming feeling of grief." This comment reflects what is commonly called a "grief attack." Another way of describing an episode like this is "memory embraces." A grief attack or memory embrace is a period of time when you may have intense anxiety and sharp pain.

Grief attacks are normal. When and if one strikes you, be compassionate with yourself. You have every right to miss the person who has died and to feel temporary paralysis. Whatever you do, don't try to deny a grief attack when you experience it. It is probably more powerful than you are.

My experience with grief attacks or memory embraces is or has been...

Anniversary or Holiday Grief Occasions.
Naturally, anniversary and holiday occasions can bring about "pangs" of grief. Birthdays, wedding dates, holidays, and special occasions create a heightened sense of loss. At these times, you may likely experience a grief attack or memory embrace. Plan ahead when you know some naturally painful times are coming for you. Unfortunately, some bereaved people will not mention anniversaries, holidays, or special occasions to anyone. As a result, they suffer in silence, and their feelings of isolation increase.

My experience with anniversary and holiday grief occasions is or has been...

Sudden Mood Changes. When your pet dies, you may feel like you are surviving one minute and in the depths of despair the next. Sudden changes in your mood are a difficult, natural part of your journey. These mood changes can be small or very dramatic. They can be triggered by driving past a familiar place, a song, an insensitive comment, or even changes in the weather.

If you have ups and downs, don't be hard on yourself. Be patient with yourself. As you do the work of mourning and move toward healing, the periods of hopelessness will be replaced by periods of hopefulness. During these times, you also can benefit from a support system that understands these mood changes as normal.

What has your experience with sudden mood changes been?

Physical Symptoms of the Pet who Died. When you care deeply about a pet and they die, you sometimes develop ways to identify with and feel close to that pet. One way is by relating to the physical symptoms of the pet who died. For example, if it died from a brain tumor you may have frequent headaches. If he died of a heart attack, you may have chest pains. Of course, you need to have a physician check your symptoms, but also be aware that you might be experiencing identification symptoms of physical illness.

My experience with identifying with my pet's illness is or has been...

Dreams. Dreaming about the pet in your life who has died may be a part of your grief journey. If it is, remember that no one is a better expert than you are in understanding what your dreams mean to you.

Dreams are one of the ways the work of mourning takes place. They may or may not play an important part in your experience. Find someone who will not interpret your dreams but will let you describe them.

Some of the dreams that I have had about my pet are...

Coping with Pet Loss

Take care of your body. The body is the container of the mind which is now feeling intense emotion. Nurturing it in the following ways will ease your grieving process.

> *Nutrition: eat healthy meals even if
> your appetite is reduced.
> *Sleep: be sure to get at least 5-8 hours
> daily, no more, no less.
> *Exercise: even walking will help your
> mood in this difficult time.

Talk to people who can empathize with your grief. Consistent interaction and sharing with those you feel comfortable around will be most beneficial.

Maintain structure in your life by continuing to do the activities you did before the loss, with the exception of those you did with or for your pet. Do not allow this major disruption to snowball into every aspect of your life. Structure will help your regain your bearings.

Perform a ritual when you feel the time is right.

When Your Pet Dies

Some have funerals at a pet cemetery or memorials with friends and family. Others may create a small shrine for a brief time.

Allow yourself to feel sadness and loss. Grief is a normal response to a normal occurrence, yet each person goes through it differently. If you feel as though you cannot recover, or it you have thoughts of self-harm, contact a mental health professional immediately.

Anyone who has had a pet for any length of time knows how painful it is when that beloved pet reaches the end of his or her time here with us. We are often left with questions, anger, guilt, or an overwhelming sense of loss that we are sometimes unable to cope with. Very often, sharing these feelings with others who will understand is the first step toward healing. Discussing them and realizing we are not alone helps us find strength and solace. We begin the healing process which will allow us to cherish the memories of our pets and recall them with fondness. It allows the pain to start to diminish and gives us permission to continue to love and concentrate on those still with us.

Share your feelings now, either about your own pet, or help console those who need it.

How Am I Doing?

The process of healing in your grief calls on all of your personal resources. As you know by now, grief and mourning are powerful experiences. So is your ability to help yourself heal. In doing the work of mourning, you are moving toward healing. Some people may tell you to "get over" your grief. Don't listen to them. As a human being, you don't "get over" grief. You live with it and work to reconcile yourself to it.

A number of models are used to describe grief: resolution, recovery, re-establishment, or re-organization are a few of these models. These words suggest a total return to your normal life or the life you experienced before the death of someone loved. Yet in my experience, everyone is changed forever by the grief journey.

Yes, you are changed. The death of your pet alters your life forever. The issue is not that you will never be happy again. It is simply that you will never be exactly the same as you were before the death. In exploring what your ultimate healing goal will be, I want you to consider using the term "reconciliation." I believe that this term is more expressive of what occurs as you work to integrate the new reality of moving forward in life without the physical presence of the person who has died.

As you embrace your grief and do the work of mourning you can realize your progress by answering the following questions:

* Have you recognized the reality and finality of the death of your pet?

* Have you returned to stable eating and sleeping patterns that were present prior to the death?

* Do you have a renewed sense of release or relief from the pet who has died? You will have thoughts about the pet, but you will not be preoccupied with these thoughts.

* Have you rediscovered the capacity to enjoy experiences in life that are normally enjoyable?

* Have you established new and healthy relationships?

When Your Pet Dies

* Do you have the capacity to organize and plan your life toward the future?

* Do you have the capacity to live a full life without feelings of guilt or regret?

* Do you have the capacity to become comfortable with the way things are rather than attempting to make things like they were?

* Do you have the capacity to welcome more change in your life?

* Do you have an awareness that you have allowed yourself to fully grieve, and you have survived?

* Do you have a sense of a new reality, meaning and purpose in your life?

* Have you discovered new parts of your personality sense the death of your pet?

* Do you have the capacity to be compassionate with yourself when normal recurrences of intense grief occur?

* Do you have the capacity to acknowledge that the pain of loss is an inherent part of life resulting from the ability to give and receive love?

Other Places to Find Support

If you feel that time is passing too painfully for you or you want some very special and caring support, there are many sources of support available to you.

Your veterinarian. Your relationship with your veterinarian has just been very emotional and personal. Few people understand your loss like the staff who have cared for your pet and who have helped you make your decision. Some pet owners, when going through the anger stage of grief will blame their veterinarian for their loss. Talk this over with your pet's caregiver; it may help you come to terms with that part of your loss.

Church or Synagogue. If you have a relationship with a pastor or rabbi, don't forget that they may be there for you. For many people, religion is a framework of life. Don't think that they would not want to hear that you lost your pet.

Counseling. Seeking professional help is absolutely all right and very common. Grief and depression are just as real over the loss of a pet as they are over the loss of a person. Some professionals offer pet loss support groups. At a group like this you will be with other people in the same situation as you who understand your grief and can share your experiences.

Friends and family. Don' t overlook this resource. Many of them have been with you in your grief from the time of decision or the receipt of the terrible news. And most have known your pet as long as you have. It may be difficult to accept help, but if someone offers, think about accepting it.

Remember, with time your pain will lessen and the wounds of despair will heal. You will never forget your beloved pet; the many happy memories will always be with you.

Helping Friends Who Are Mourning a Loss

Sue, a 79-year-old widow, came home from shopping to find the front door of her house smashed in by a burglar. As upsetting as this was, she had another terrible surprise awaiting her. Her cherished parrot Petey - her companion for nearly 40 years - was missing from his opened cage. "I'm surprised I didn't have a heart attack right on the spot!" she remembered, with anguish in her voice. How would you go about trying to help Sue?

When people think of pet loss they usually think of an animal dying. But there are many different types of loss and no matter how the loss occurs, the guardians of these pets often have intense reactions as a result. They may experience distress, anxiety, guilt, depression, sadness, loneliness, and other unpleasant feelings for quite some time after. How you talk to them about their feelings and reactions can make an important difference in their lives.

Some people do not take pet loss seriously. They think people are silly for grieving over a pet. They are quick to tell you to get on with your life and get another animal. They cannot understand how you can become so attached to a dog, cat, bird, or other pet. Out of fear of being put down or ridiculed, many animal lovers keep their strong feelings of attachment to their pets - and their grief in relation to them - to themselves. They are then left alone with their upsetting feelings of bereavement. This is not healthy.

As a pet loss counselor, I am frequently asked by concerned people what to say to bereaved pet "owners." Most people who have had an animal companion die - or have lost their valued relationship in some other way - appreciate these responses:

Adopt an attitude that conveys that you are taking the distressing experience of the mourner seriously. Listen and speak with empathy, understanding, support, sensitivity and compassion.

Show interest by asking the mourner about the circumstances of the pet's death/loss.

Convey that you welcome hearing the stories of his/her fond memories of her/his animal friend. Ask how the pet got his or her name, and encourage the mourner to tell you how the pet became a member of the family.

Refrain from asking if the mourner is planning on getting another pet, or suggesting where such a pet might be bought. A pet owner might feel offended by this - despite your good intentions in asking.

Avoid the use of clichés - such as telling the mourner that time heals all wounds, or reassuring them that they will soon "get over it."

Send the mourner a condolence card - one specifically made for pet loss, if you can find one and if it seems appropriate. Writing a thoughtful line or two (or more) on the card, in your own words, will probably be very much appreciated.

Write down the dates that are important to the bereaved pet owner, like the dates of the pet's death, birth, adoption, etc. Consider sending a follow-up note, e-mail, or card, or making a telephone call to the mourner in remembrance of these special days.

Send a donation, in honor of the deceased or lost pet, to an animal-related organization (such as a humane society, animal shelter, or one devoted to improving the health of animals through medical research).

After a few weeks or months, follow up by asking the bereaved individual how she or he is doing in his/her mourning process over the loss of her/his pet. (Use the pet's name and correct gender).

Be cautious about making assumptions on how you think the mourner might be feeling and reacting. Realize that the mourning process, as with people's responses to the death of human loved ones, can be multi-layered and highly complex. Keep in mind that everyone is unique, with her/his own needs and preferences. Good judgment is essential in dealing with people in such a vulnerable state.

Encourage the mourner to talk to a professional if their grief is prolonged or especially intense. Psychotherapists who specialize in pet loss counseling provide a supportive, compassionate, and knowledgeable presence to anyone grieving the loss of a pet.

Children and Pet Loss

The death of a cherished pet creates a sense of loss for adults and produces a predictable chain of emotions. The stages of grief are typically denial, sadness, depression, guilt, anger, and, finally, relief (or recovery). However, the effects on children vary widely depending upon the child's age and maturity level. The basis for their reaction is their ability to understand death.

Two and Three Year Olds

Children who are two or three years old typically have no understanding of death. They often consider it a form of sleep. They should be told that their pet has died and will not return. Common reactions to this include temporary loss of speech and generalized distress. The two or three year old should be reassured that the pet's failure to return is unrelated to anything the child may have said or done. Typically, a child in this age range will readily accept another pet in place of the dead one.

Four, Five, and Six Year Olds

Children in this age range have some understanding of death but in a way that relates to a continued existence. The pet may be considered to be living underground while continuing to eat, breathe, and play. Alternatively, it may be considered asleep. A return to life may be expected if the child views death as temporary. These children often feel that any anger they had for the pet may be responsible for its death. This view should be refuted because they may also translate this belief to the death of family members in the past. Some children also see death as contagious and begin to fear that their own death (or that of others) is imminent. They should be reassured that their death is not likely. Manifestations of grief often take the form of disturbances in bladder and bowel control, eating, and sleeping. This is best managed by parent-child discussions that allow the child to express feelings and concerns. Several brief discussions are generally more productive than one or two prolonged sessions.

Seven, Eight, and Nine Year Olds

The irreversibility of death becomes real to these children. They usually do not personalize death, thinking it cannot happen to themselves. However, some children may develop concerns about death of their parents. They may become very curious about death and its implications. Parents should be ready to respond frankly and honestly to questions that may arise. Several manifestations of grief may occur in these children, including the development of school problems, learning problems, antisocial behavior, hypochondriacal concerns, or aggression. Additionally, withdrawal, over attentiveness, or clinging behavior may be seen. Based on grief reactions to loss of parents or siblings, it is likely that the symptoms may not occur immediately but several weeks or months later.

Ten and Eleven Year Olds

Children in this age range generally understand death as natural, inevitable, and universal. Consequently, these children often react to death in a manner very similar to adults.

Adolescents

Although this age group also reacts similarly to adults, many adolescents may exhibit various forms of denial. This usually takes the form of a lack of emotional display. Consequently, these young people may be experiencing sincere grief without any outward manifestations.

A Pet's Prayer

Treat me kindly, my beloved master,
for no heart in all the world
is more grateful for kindness
than the loving heart of me.

Do not break my spirit with a stick
for though I should lick your hand
between the blows,
your patience and understanding
will more quickly teach me the
things you would have me do.

Speak to me often,
for your voice is the
world's sweetest music,
as you must know by the fierce
wagging of my tail when your
footstep falls upon my waiting ear.

When it is cold and wet,
please take me inside,
for I am now a domesticated animal,

When Your Pet Dies

no longer used to bitter elements.

And I ask no greater glory than the
privilege of sitting at your feet beside the hearth.

Though had you no home,
I would rather follow you
through ice and snow than
rest upon the softest pillow in the
warmest home in all the land,
for you are my
god and I am your devoted worshiper.

Keep my pan filled with fresh water,
for although I should not reproach you were it dry,
I cannot tell you when I suffer thirst.

Feed me clean food, that I may stay well,
to romp and play and do your bidding,
to walk by your side, and stand ready,
willing and able to protect you
with my life should your life be in danger.

And, beloved master,
should the great Master see fit
to deprive me of my health or sight,
do not turn me away from you.

Rather, hold me gently in your arms as skilled
hands grant me the merciful

When Your Pet Dies

boon of eternal rest and
I will leave you knowing the last
breath I drew, my fate was
ever safest in your hands.

www.ingramcontent.com/pod-product-compliance
Lightning Source LLC
Chambersburg PA
CBHW020020050426
42450CB00005B/562